The Little Book of Oracle Answers

Ivy Cahill-Davis

Cahill Davis Publishing Limited

Copyright © 2022 Ivy Cahill-Davis

The moral right of Ivy Cahill-Davis to be identified as the Author of the Work has been asserted by her in accordance with the Copyright, Designs and Patents Act 1988.

First published in Great Britain in 2022 by Cahill Davis Publishing Limited.

Apart from any use permitted under UK copyright law, this publication may only be reproduced, stored, or transmitted, in any form, or by any means, with prior permission in writing of the publishers or, in case of reprographic production, in accordance with the terms of licences issued by the Copyright Licencing Agency.

This book is intended to be used for fun only and no part of it may be interpreted as advice. The publisher and author accept no liability for any issues that may arise from the use of this book.

ISBN 978-1-7398015-7-1 (Hardback)

Cahill Davis Publishing Limited

www.cahilldavispublishing.co.uk

How to use The Little Book of Oracle Answers

A little bit of insight is sometimes all you need. With a sprinkle of advice and a little guidance, you'll be able to navigate any situation in life. Whether it's the mundane everyday decisions or a tricky situation you find yourself in, open the pages and receive the message inside.

1. Focus on the question in your mind, breathe deeply and clear your mind of everything else.
2. Flip through the book and stop when you feel called to or simply open the book on a seemingly random page.
3. The page contains the answer coming through for you.

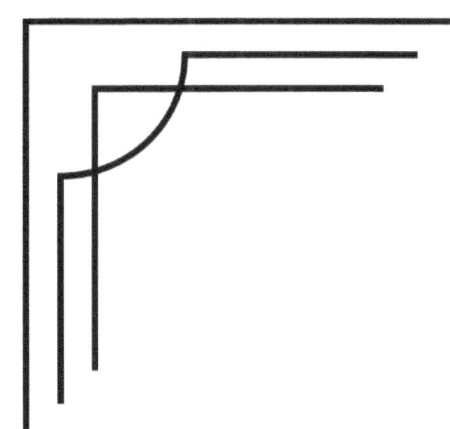

Stop daydreaming and start doing

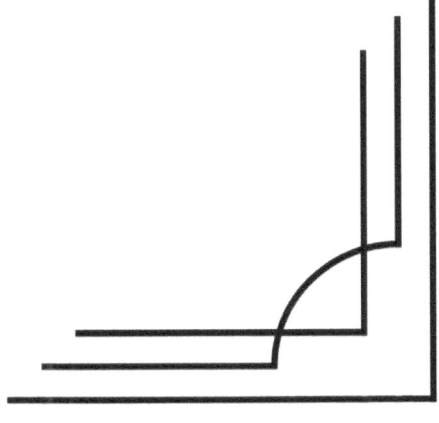

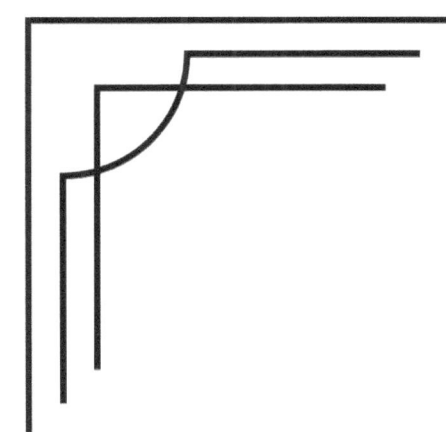

You get out what you put in

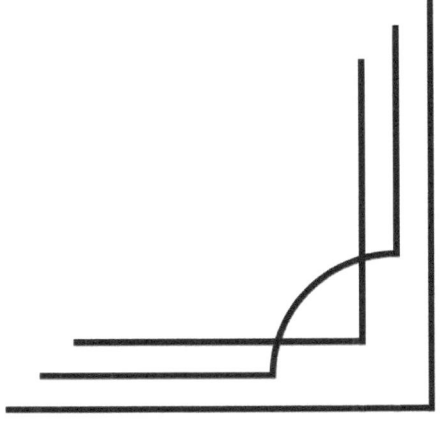

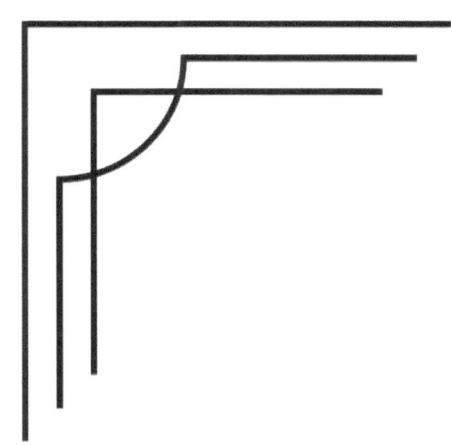

Be receptive to what's being offered to you

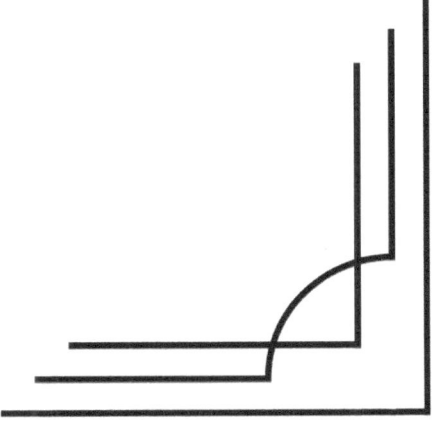

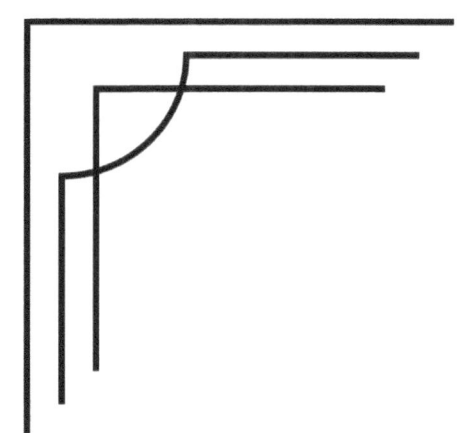

The circumstances will change very quickly

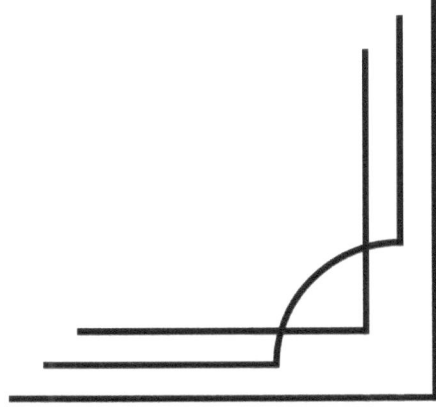

You doubt for a deeper reason but that doesn't mean it's misplaced

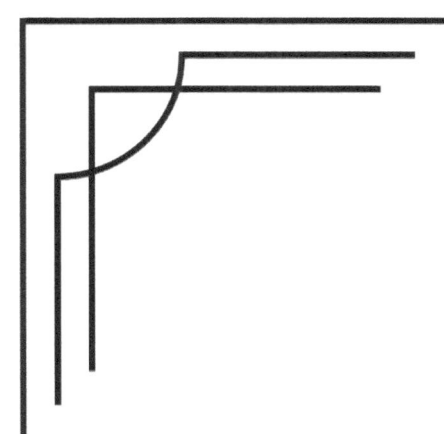

Absolutely

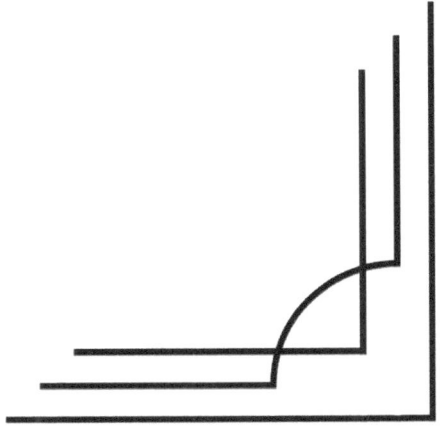

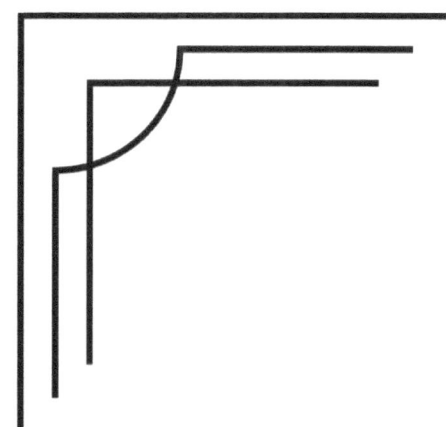

Definitely not

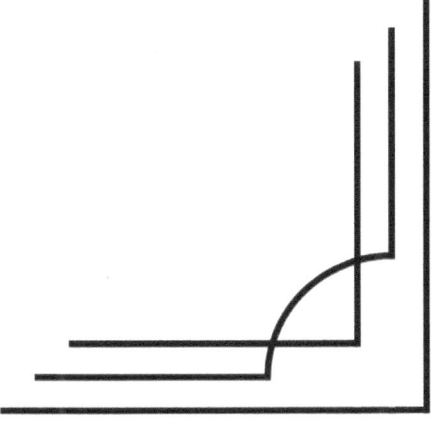

Don't allow others to use your generosity against you

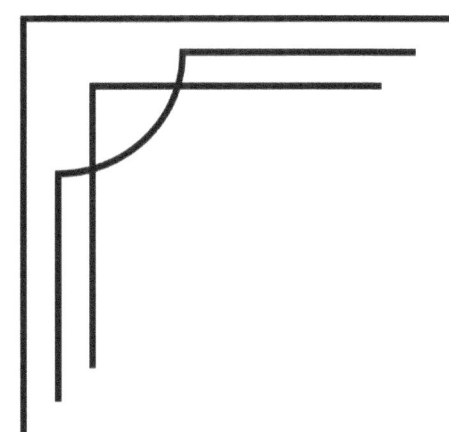

You always have a choice

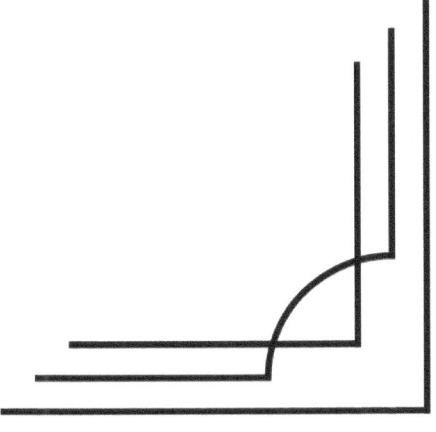

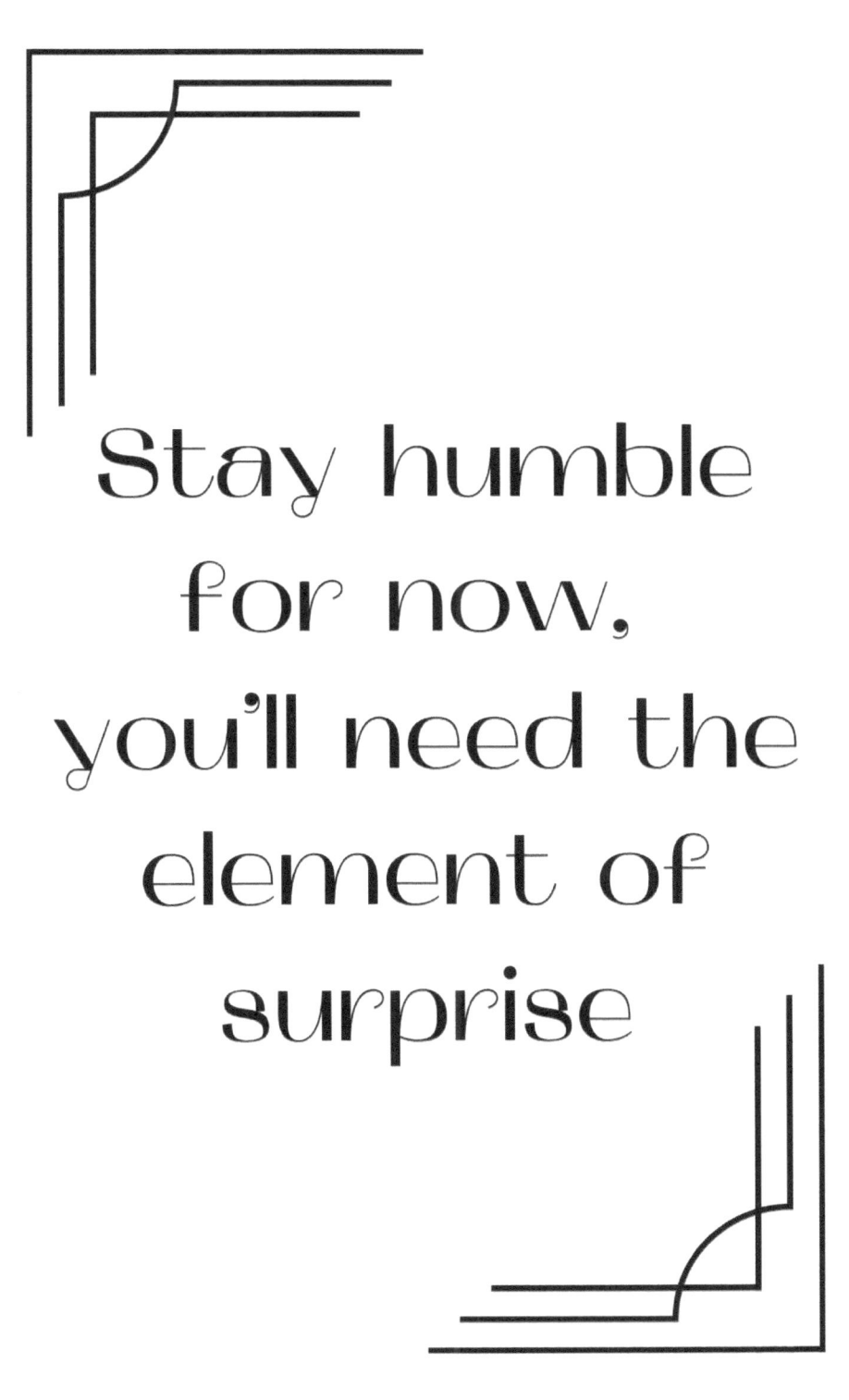

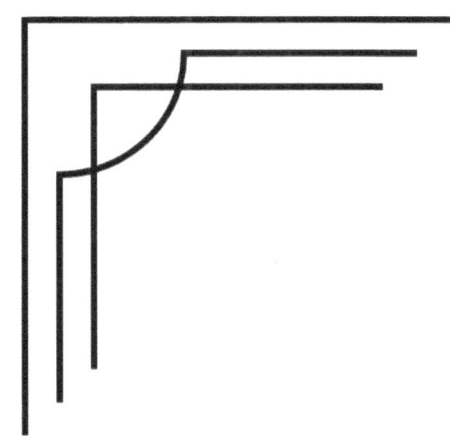

The best is
yet to come

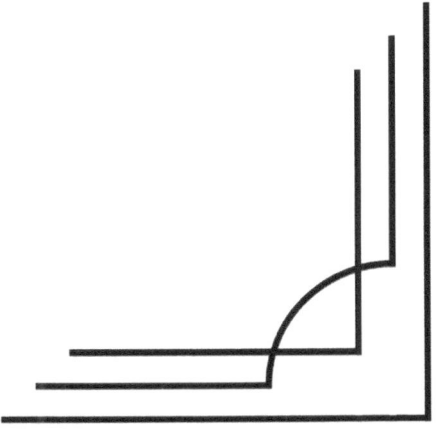

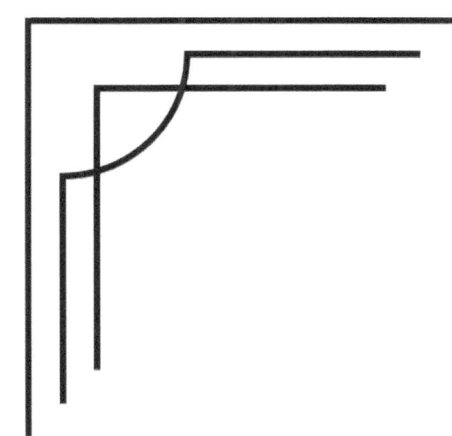

Try a little patience this time

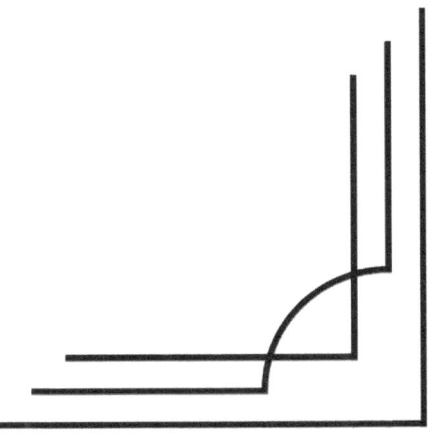

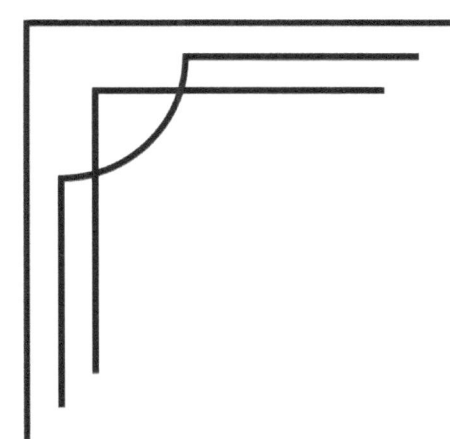

There's no reason to hold back

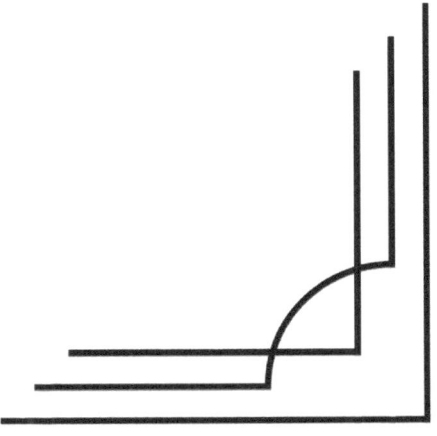

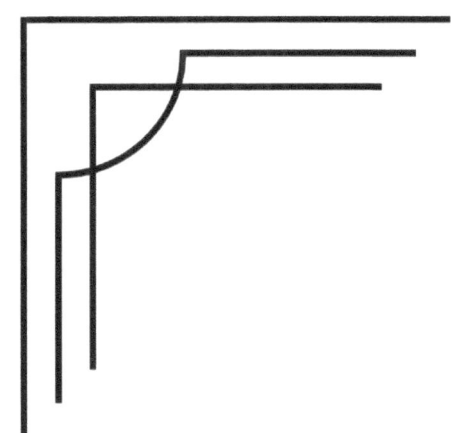

Wait a little longer

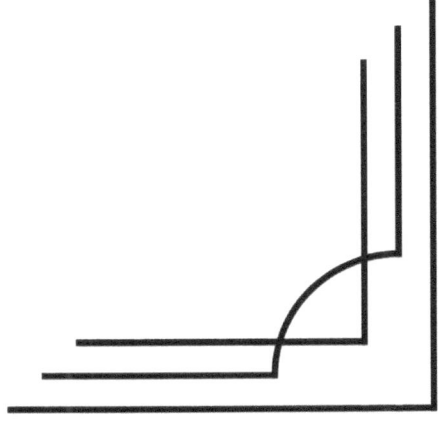

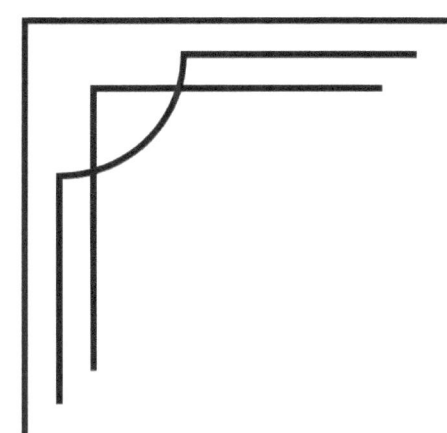

You've learnt enough, now act on what you know

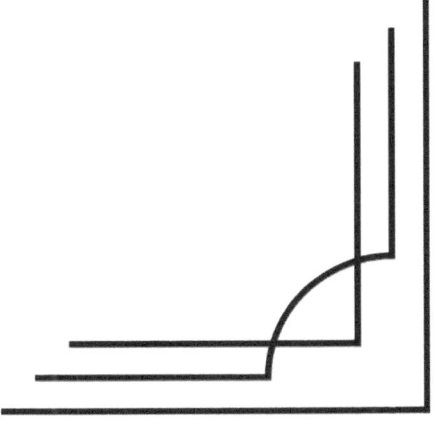

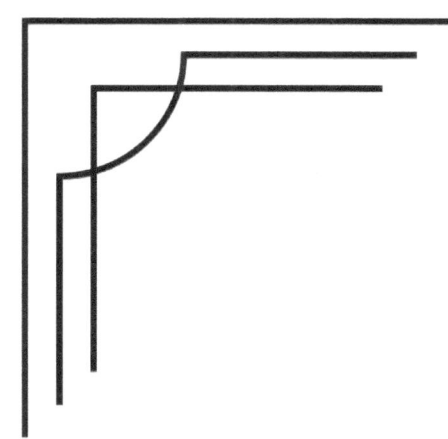

Learn more about it before you jump in

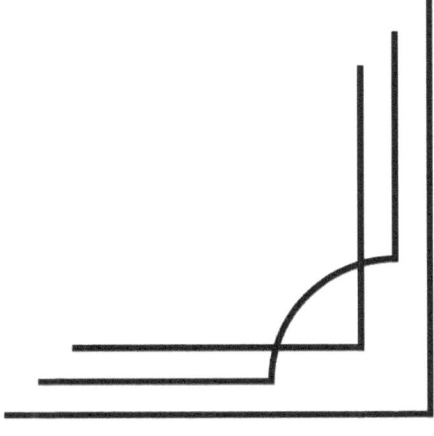

Question everything, you'll be surprised what you might learn

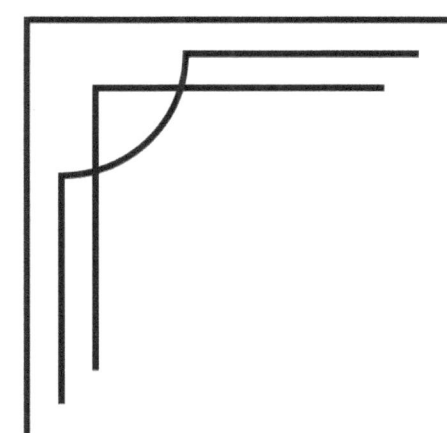

Only you are responsible for your reaction

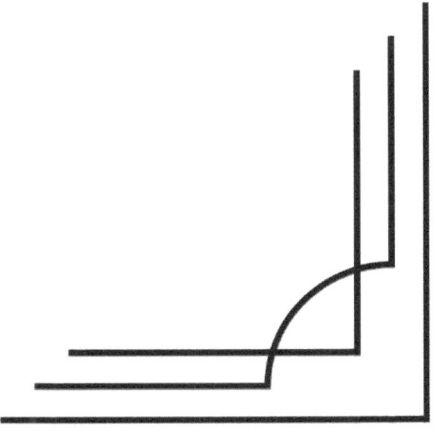

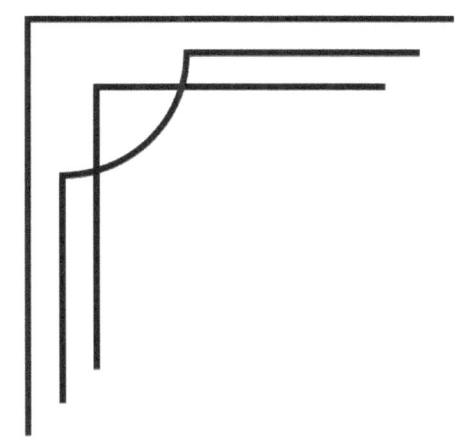

Slow down
and focus
on one thing
at a time

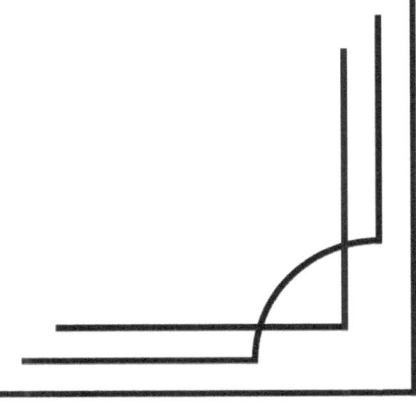

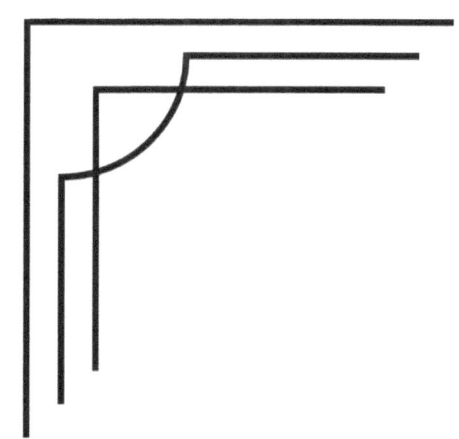

Respect yourself enough to walk away

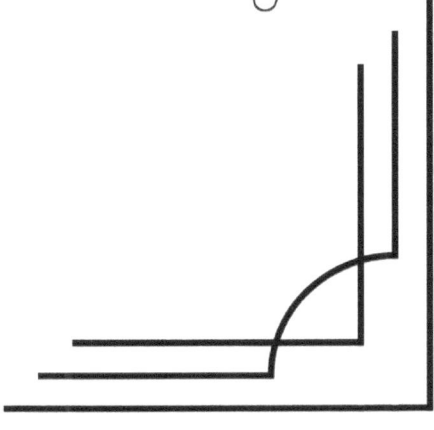

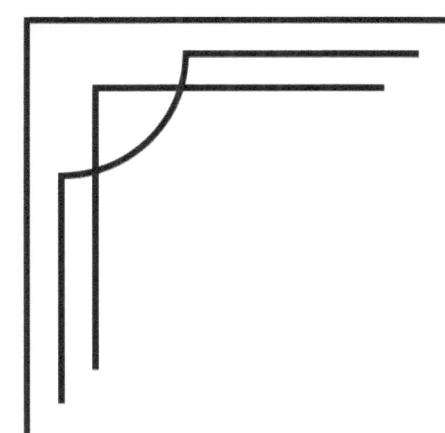

You already know the answer

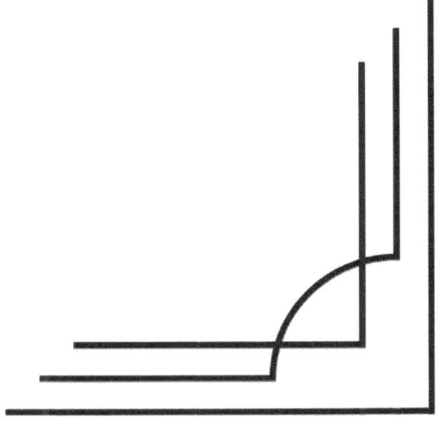

You already know what you need to do, you just need the courage to do it

There's plenty for everyone, as long as you have the confidence to take what you need

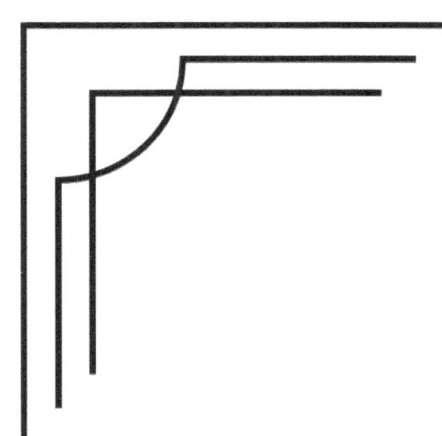

Go back to basics

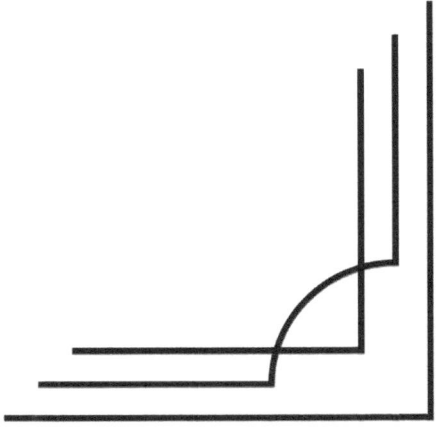

Go back to basics to spring forward even faster

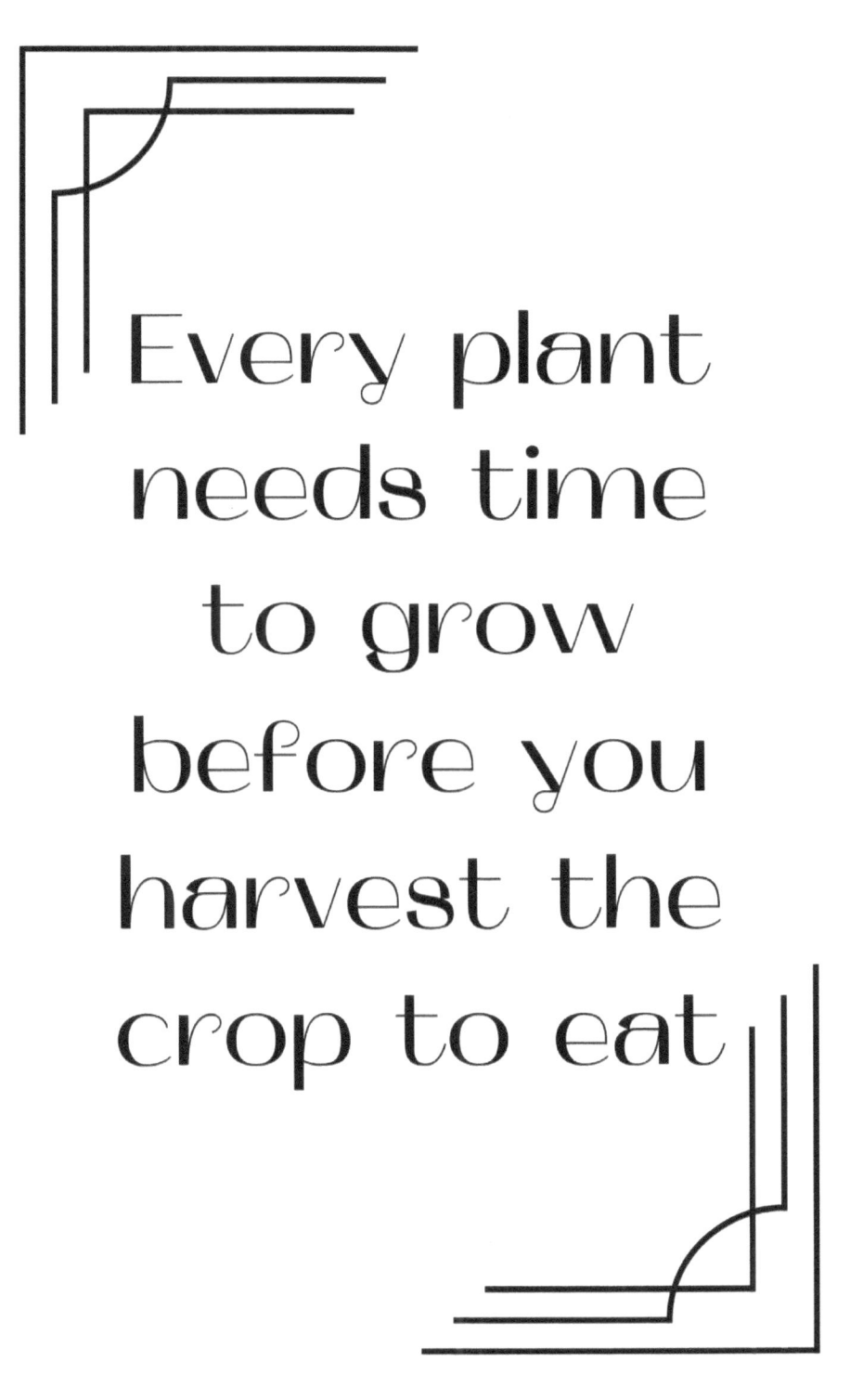
Every plant needs time to grow before you harvest the crop to eat

Sometimes you need to adapt to the situation and not adapt the situation to fit you

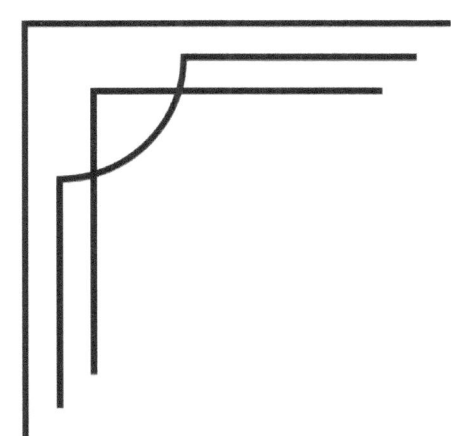

Forget it, that's where you'll find peace

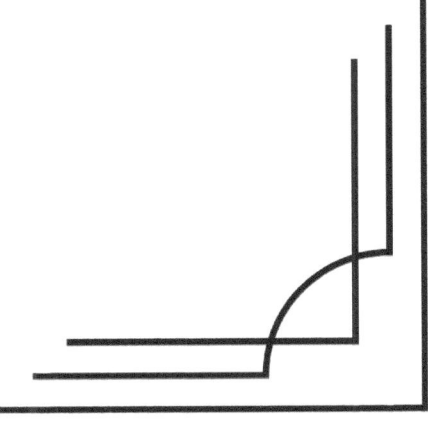

The more you know, the more you have to worry about

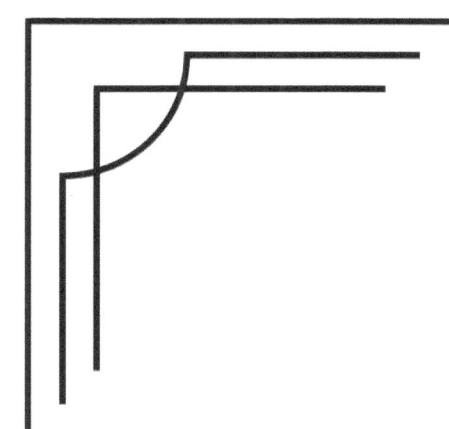

The past is behind you, leave it there

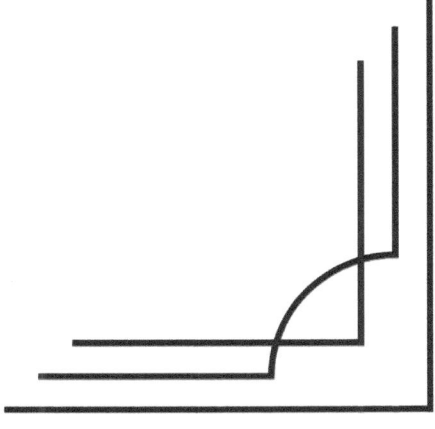

The past is worth reflecting on but don't try to live there again

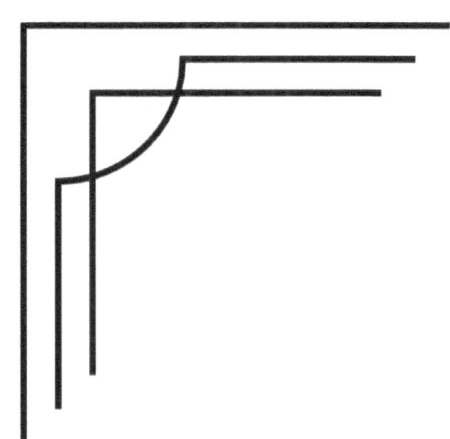

The truth is the best thing for it

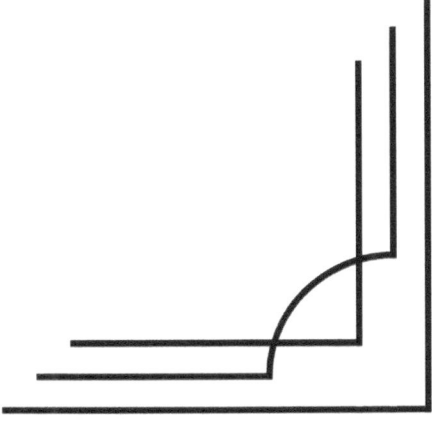

Have a plan but stay flexible, you never know where you might end up

It's either a lesson or a blessing, whether you get what you want or not

A dream is a great thing to have but you need a plan to follow to get you there

It's time to clean out the negative energy and everything that produces it

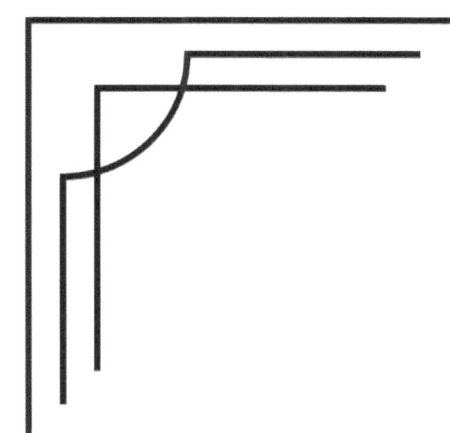

There's nothing wrong with moving on

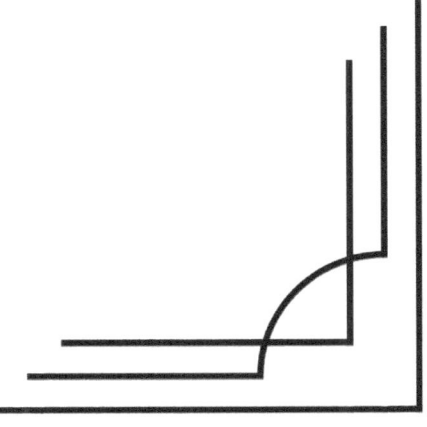

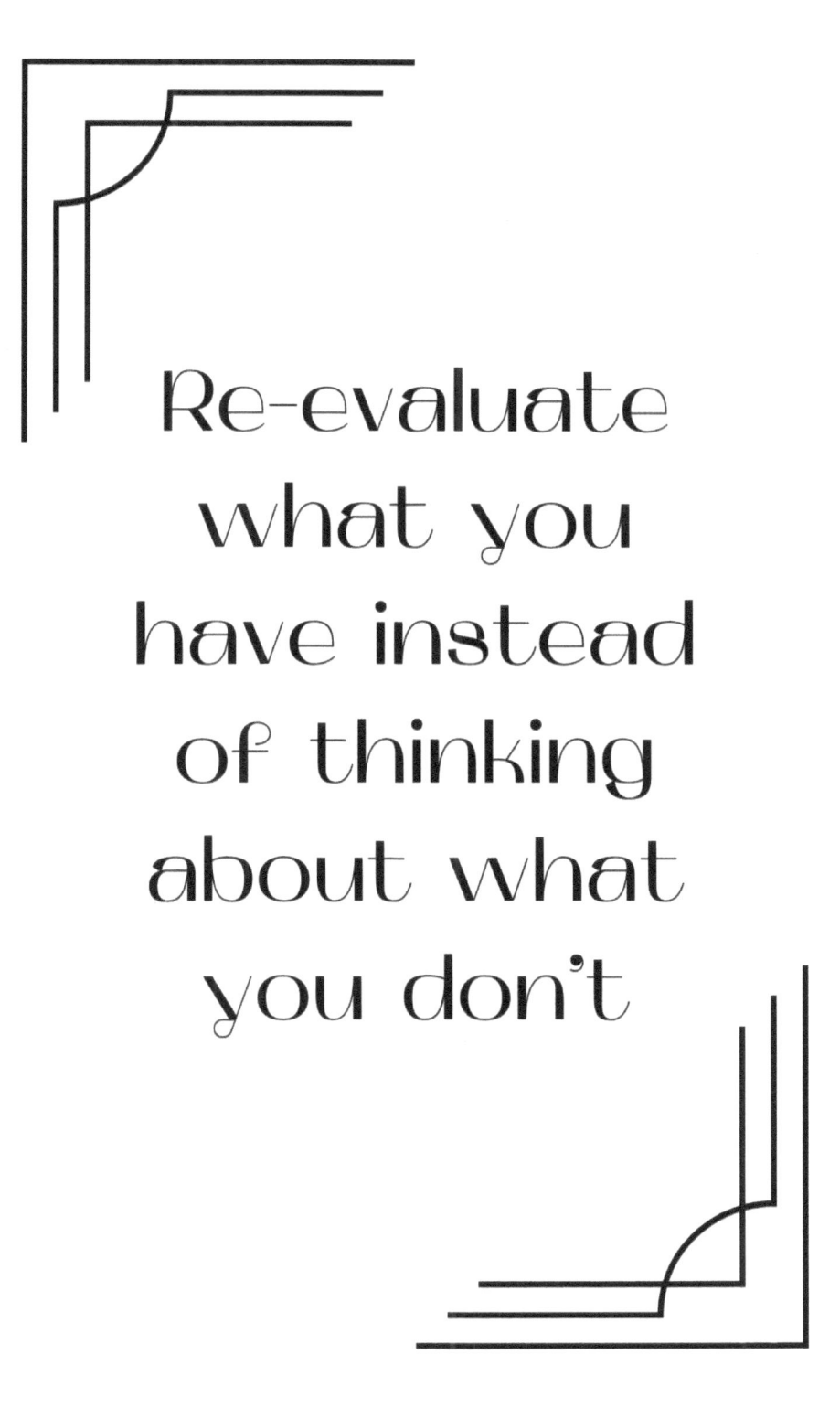

You can be a genius and still know nothing about the subject in front of you, everyone can learn more

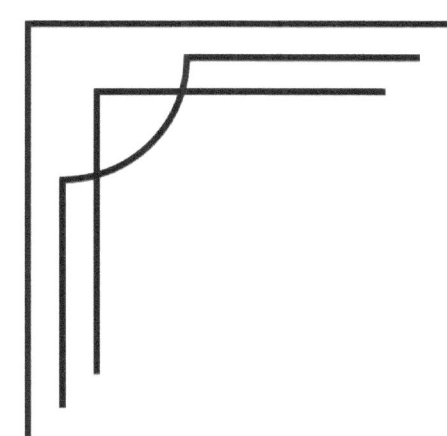

Time heals but only if you work with it

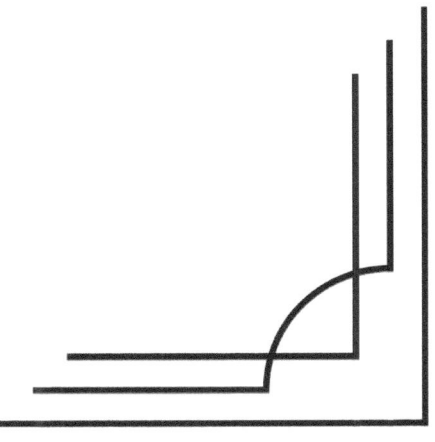

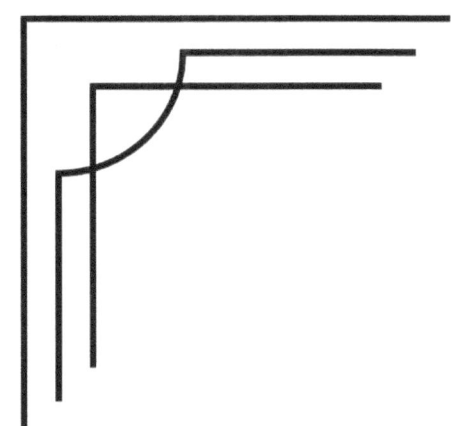

Possibility is a wonderful thing but too much can lead to procrastination

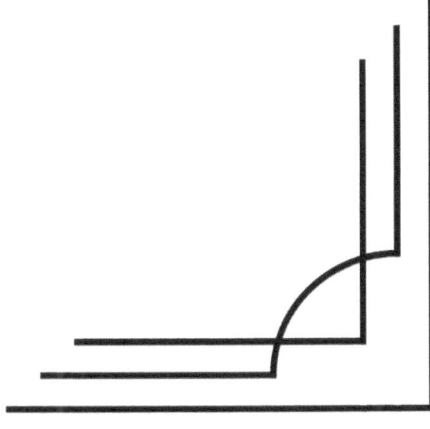

Pick one thing and go with it. You can change your mind later if you don't like where it goes

There's not much you can't achieve with a little time and focused effort

The future isn't set in stone, if you don't like where it's going then make a change now

If you know where you're going, and you want to go there, why are you wasting your time here?

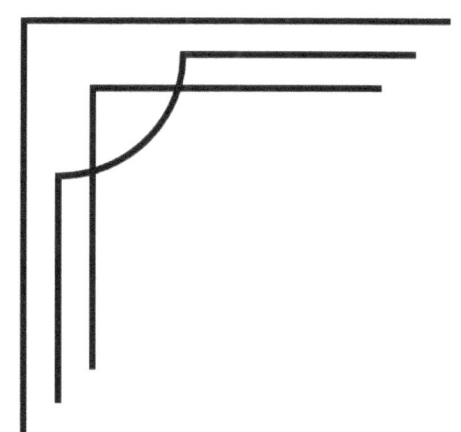

You deserve more than that

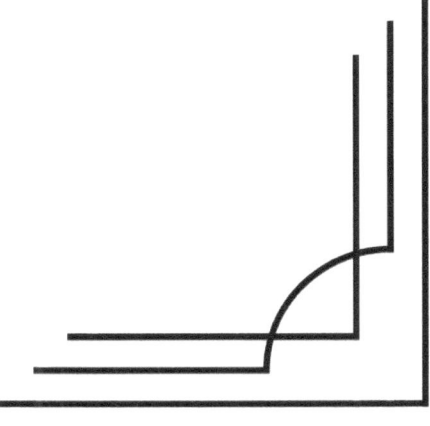

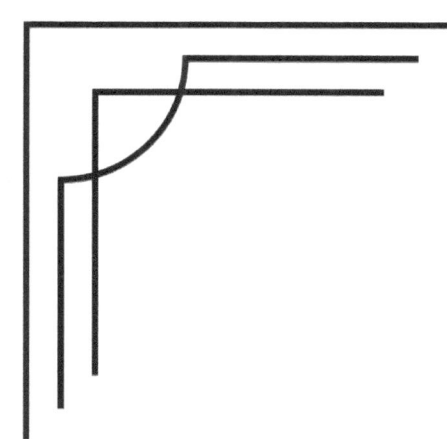

Speak up before you miss the chance

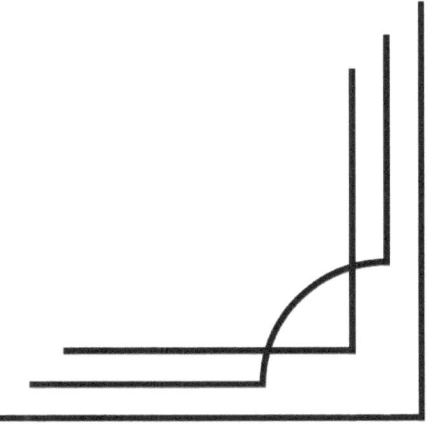

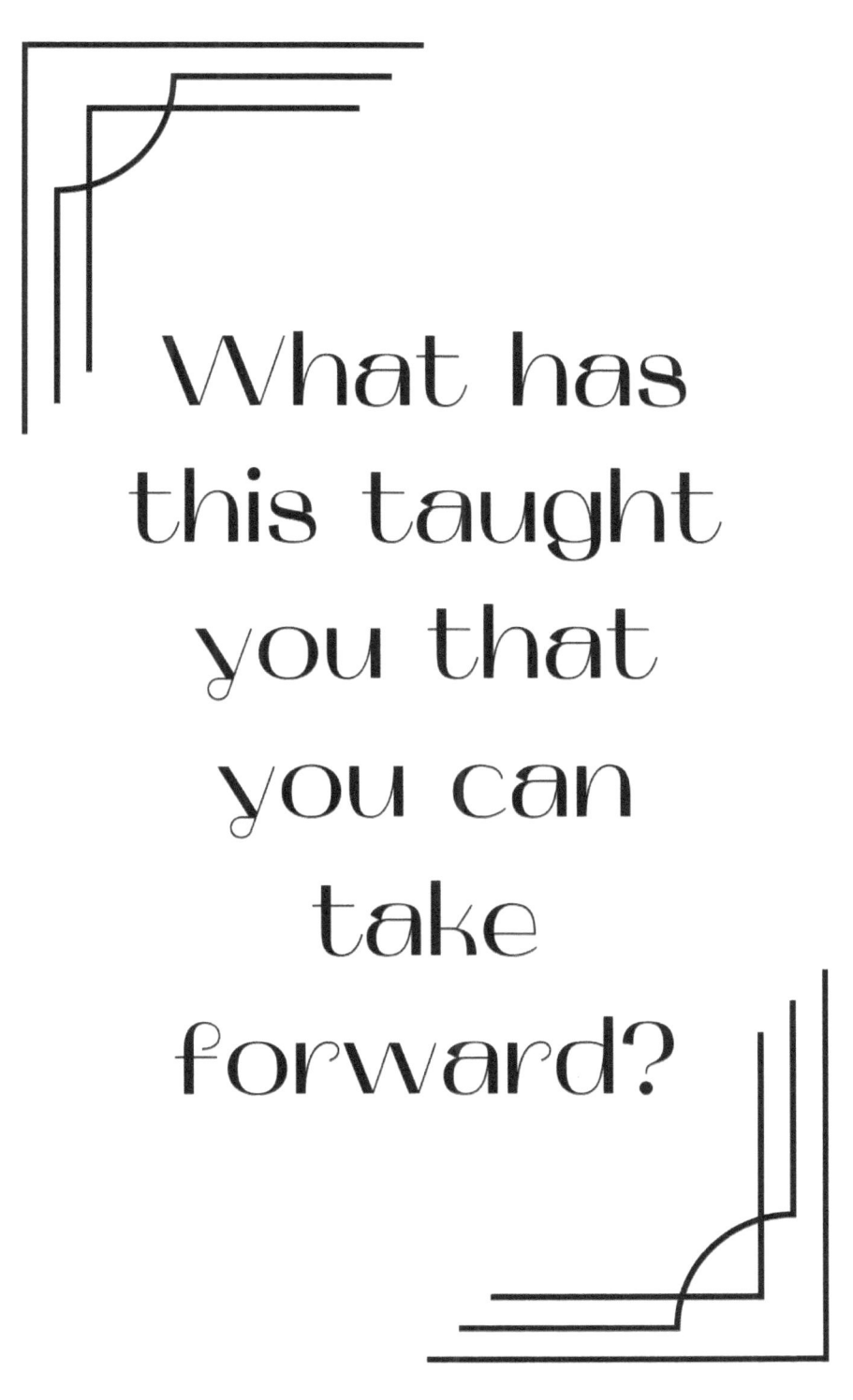

If you can't see an opportunity for yourself, create one

What do you already have and what else can you make with it?

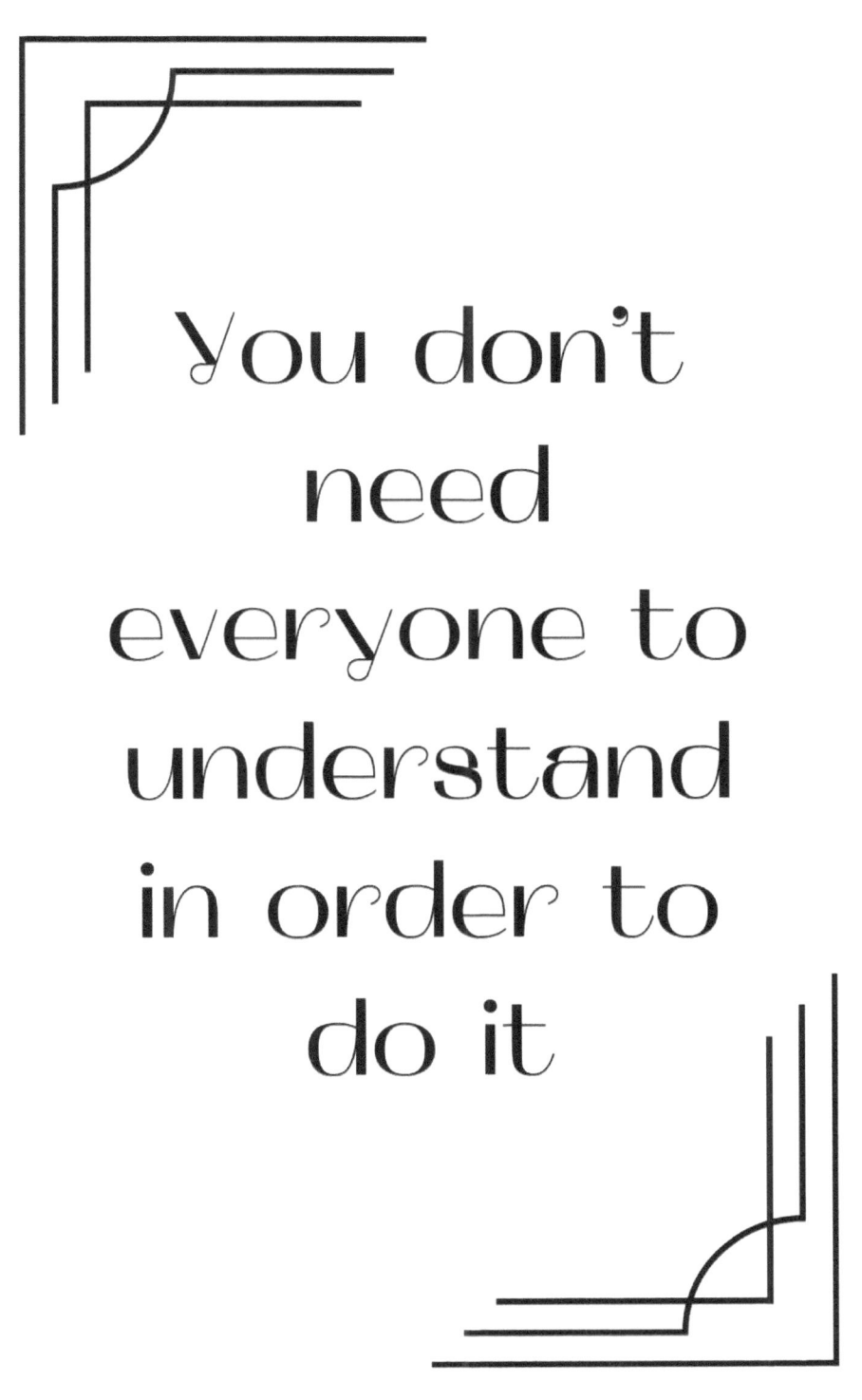

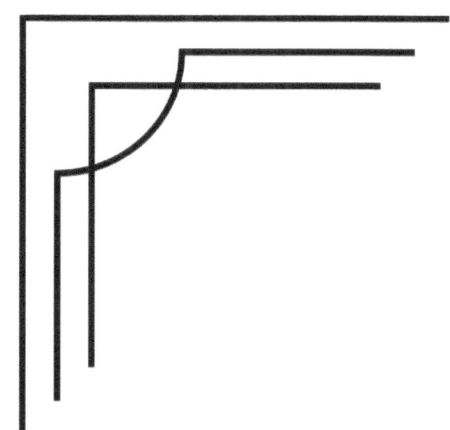

Even a 1% improvement is an improvement

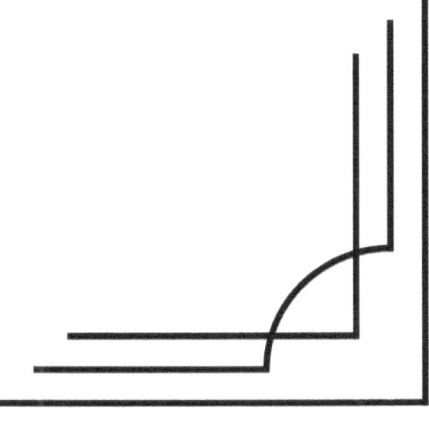

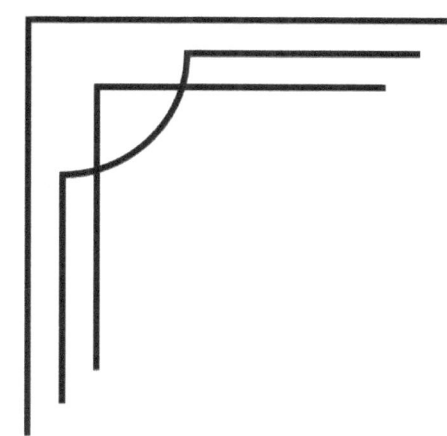

You've earned it, now enjoy it

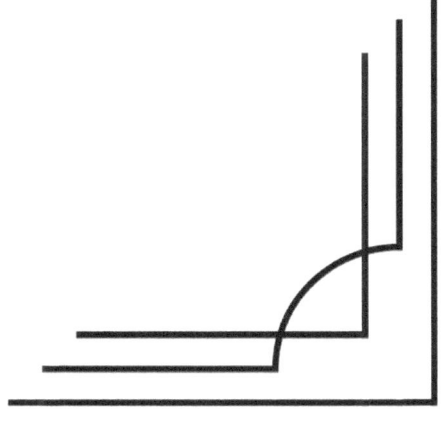

Are you choosing the familiar over the adventure?

Sometimes you have to fail in order to learn, just don't keep learning the same lesson

Did you lose it or did you let go of something you never actually had?

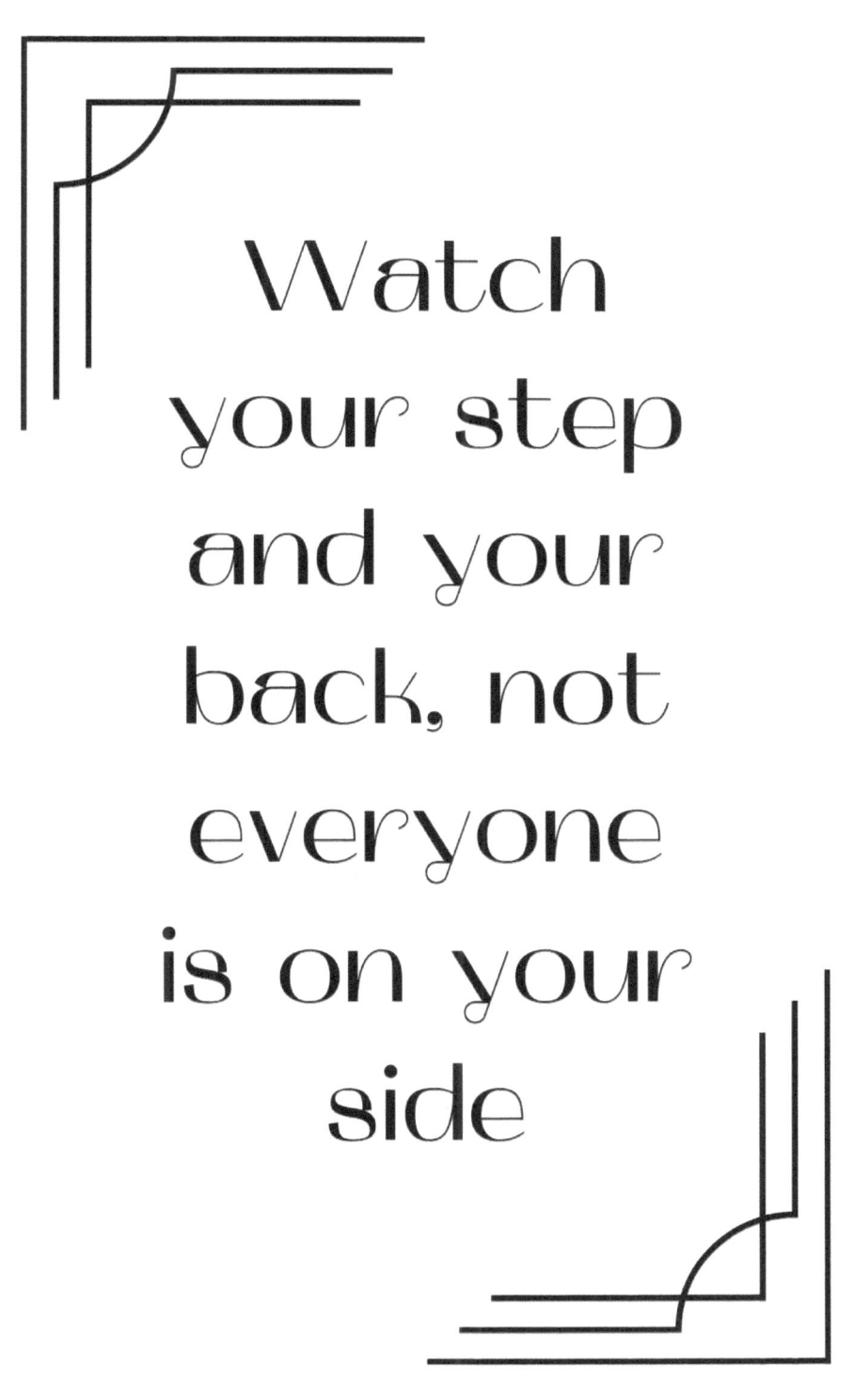

Watch your step and your back, not everyone is on your side

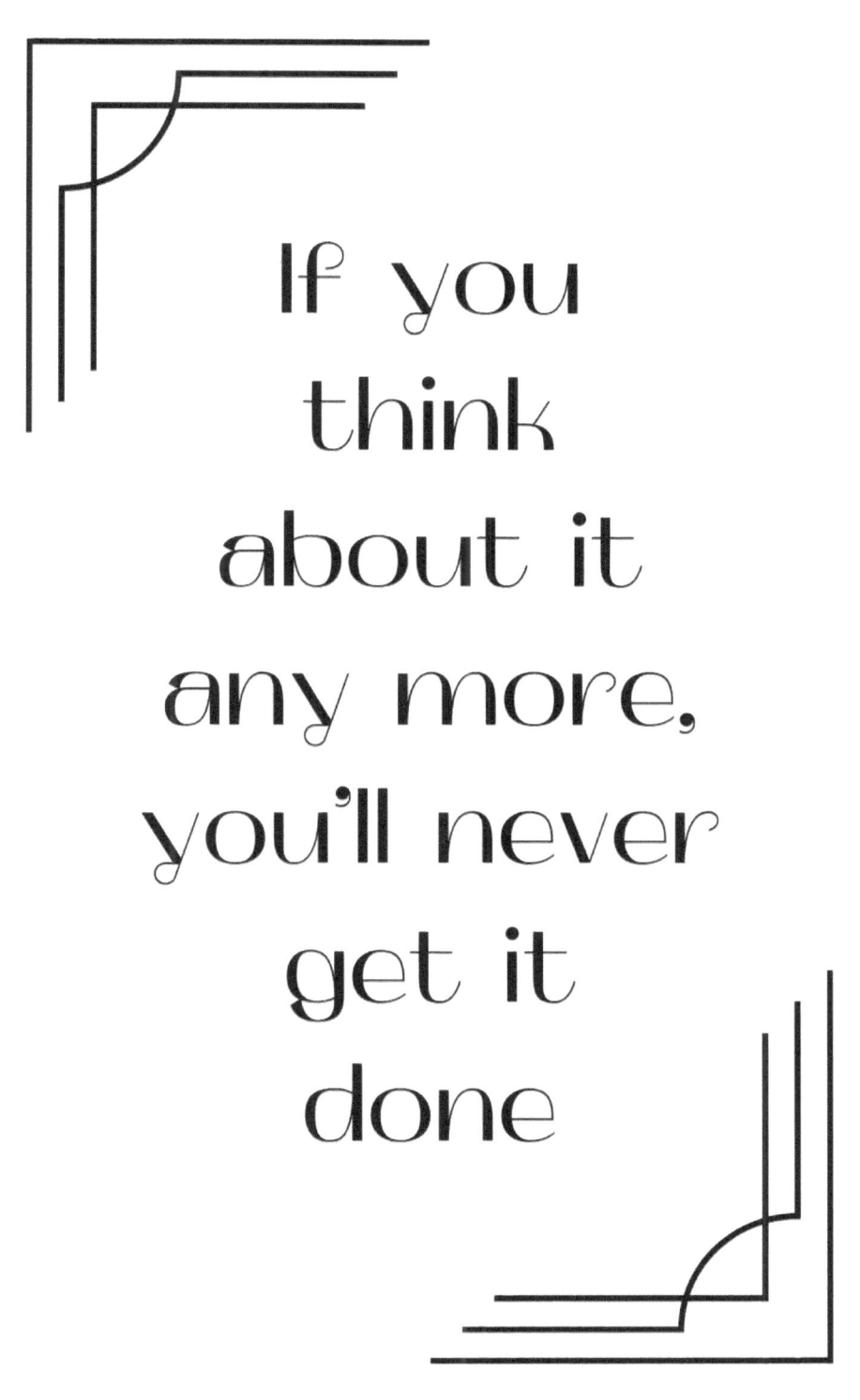

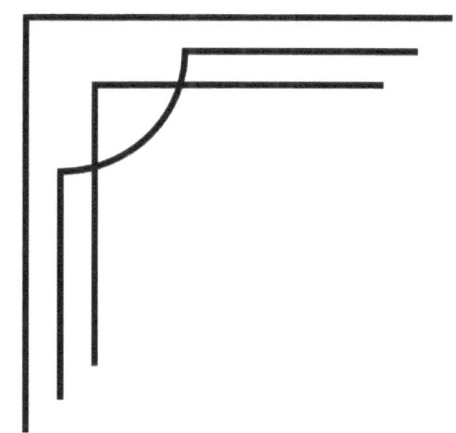

Find someone to do it with you, you'll be thankful for the companionship

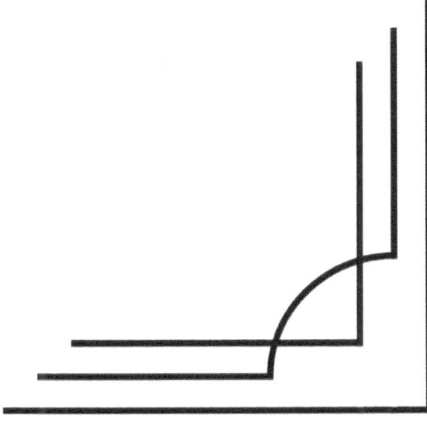

It doesn't have to be bad, stop expecting the worst

You don't have to control everything, sit back and enjoy the ride for once

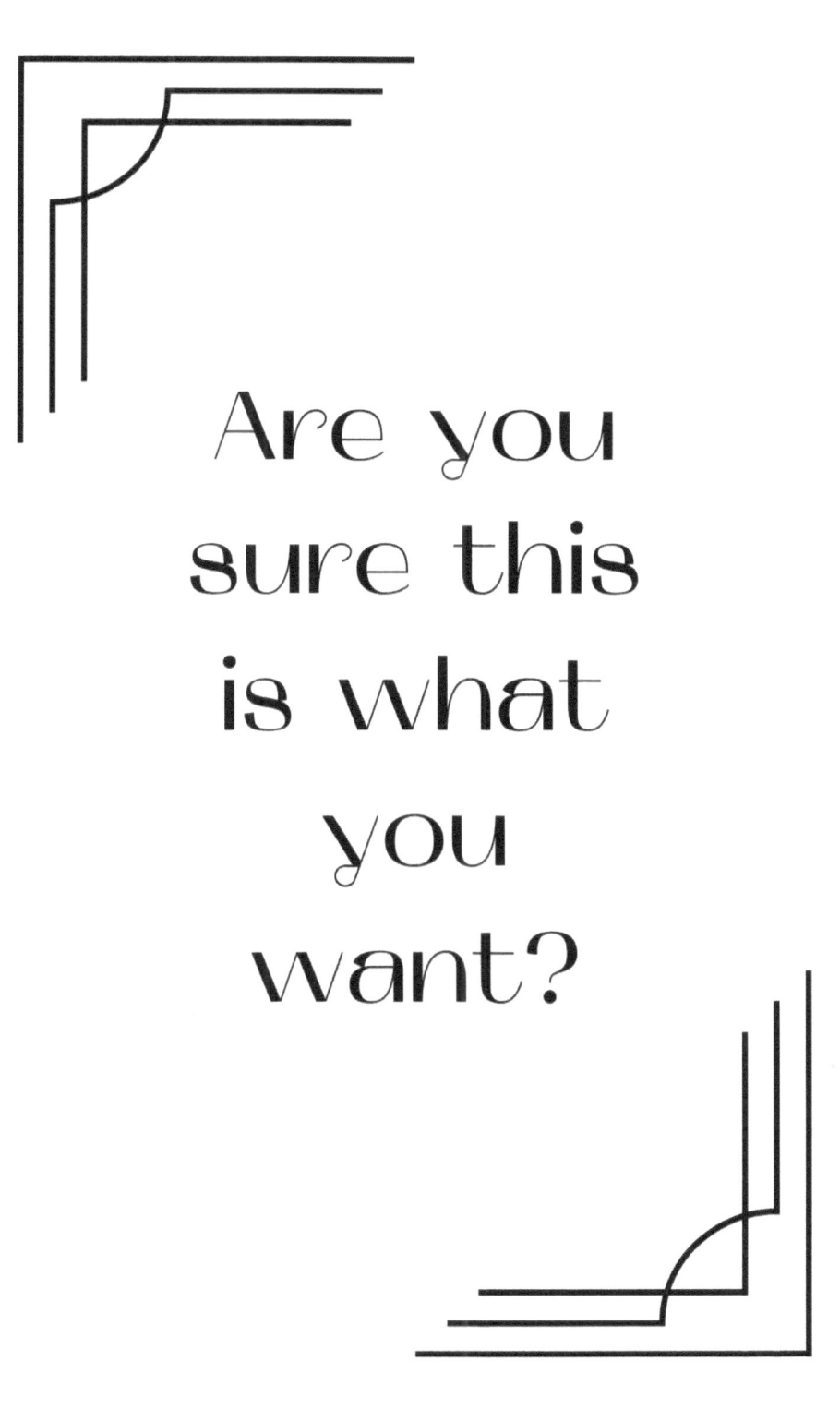

What you think you know and the truth aren't always the same thing

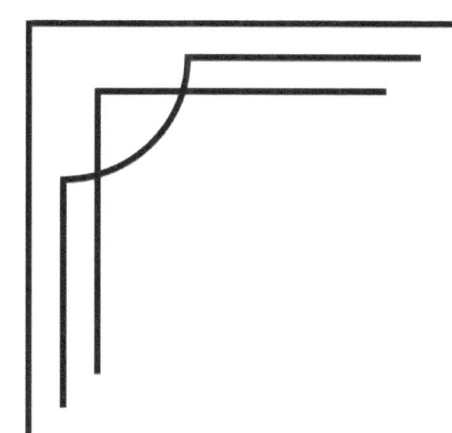

Don't
doubt the
connection
you felt

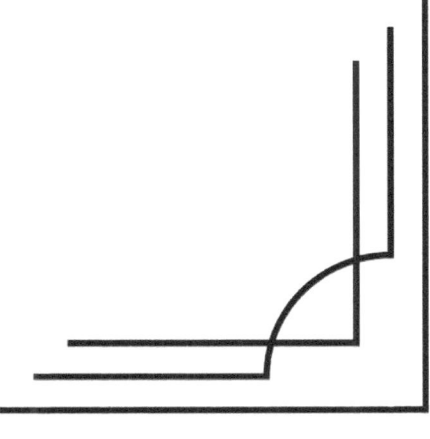

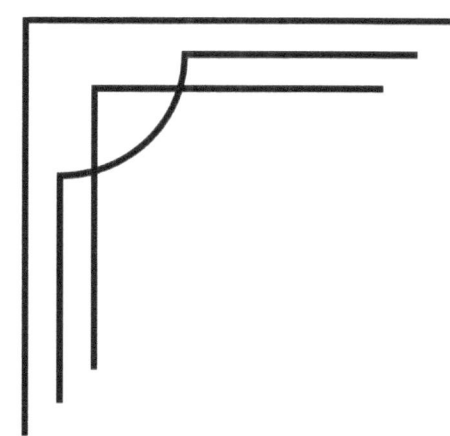

Trust your judgement on this one

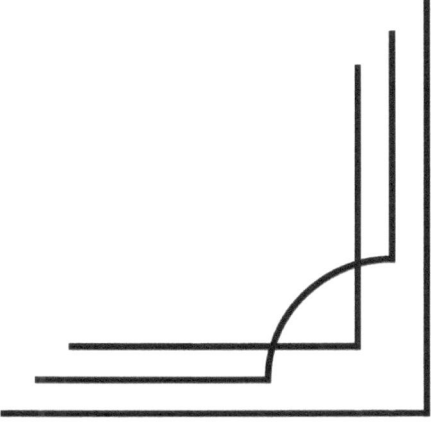

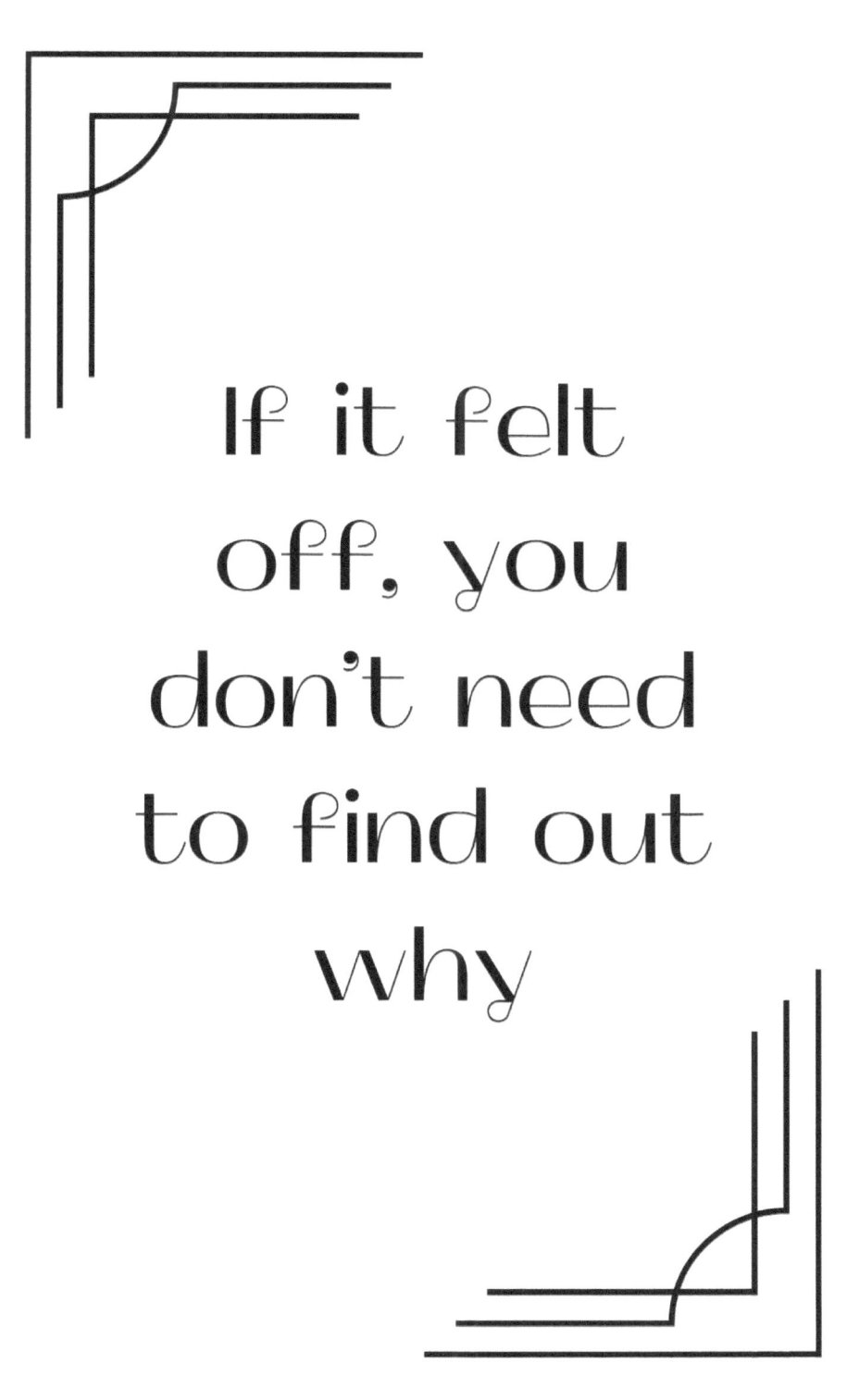

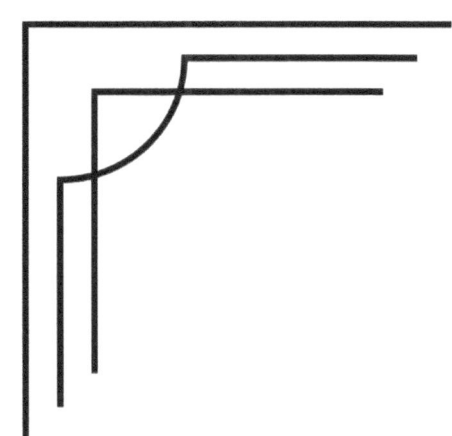

You're on the right path, keep going

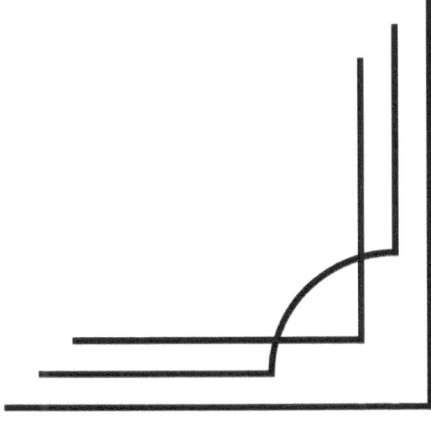

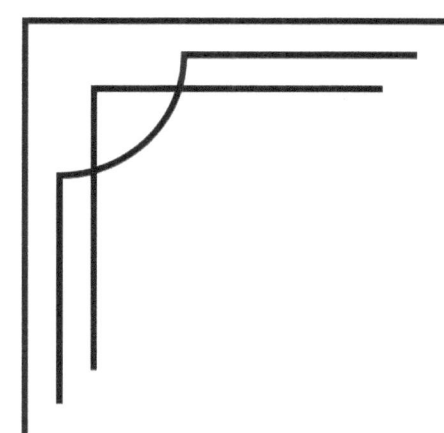

Don't stop now

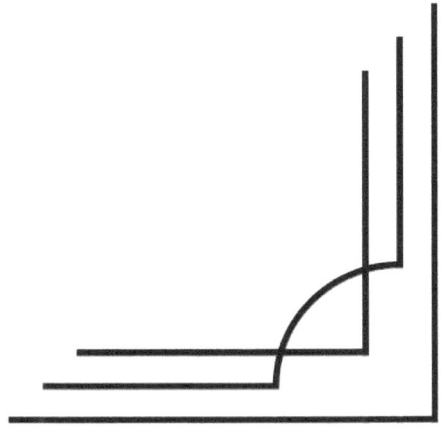

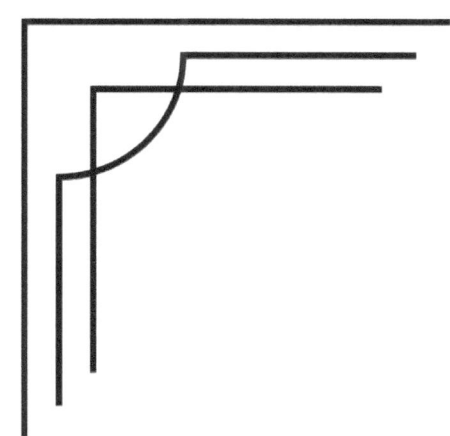

Rethink
this path

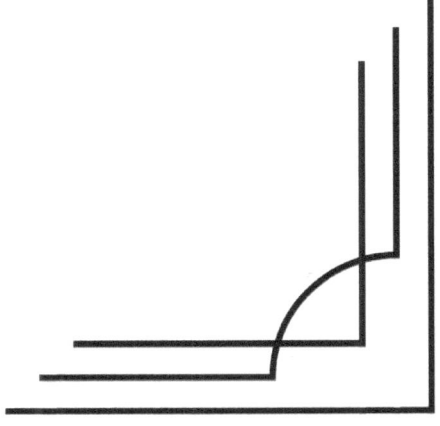

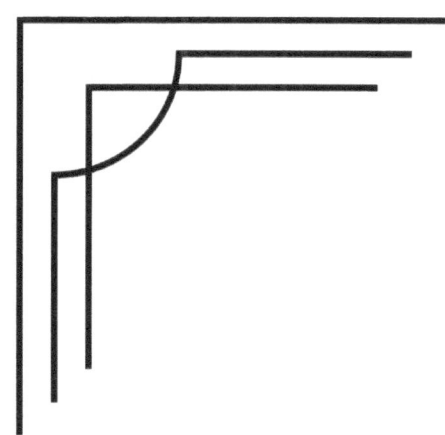

Just say yes

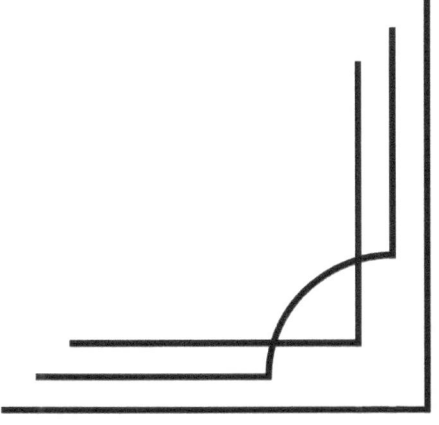

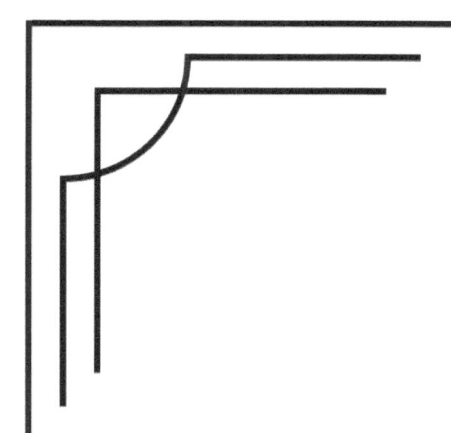

No, not now and maybe not ever

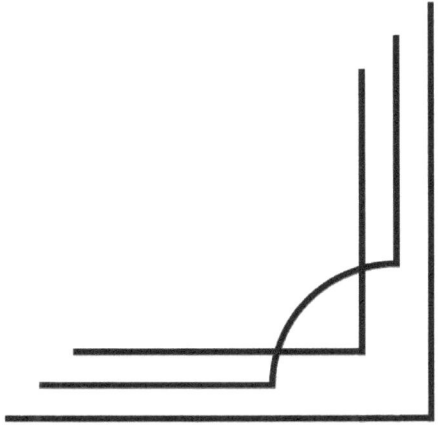

Just because that's how things have been before, doesn't mean it has to be like that in the future

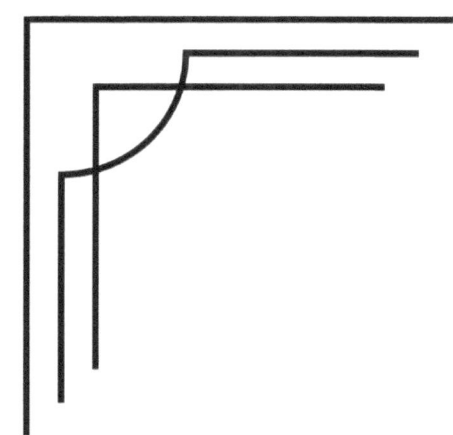

They didn't play fair but you should

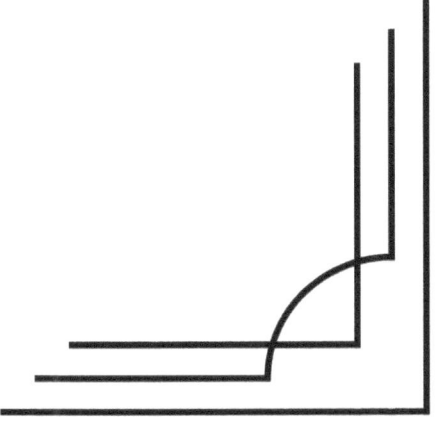

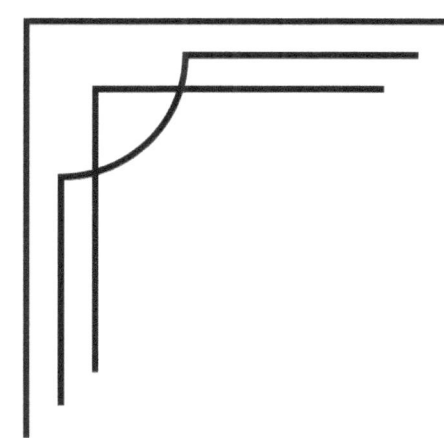

It's time to make a change

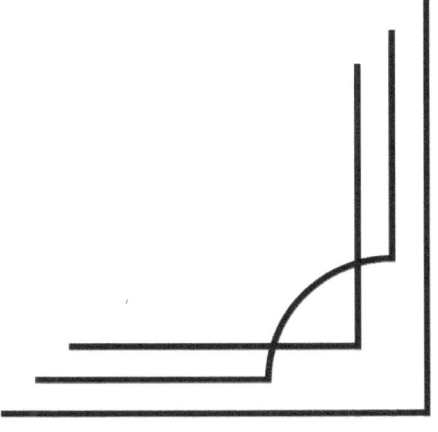

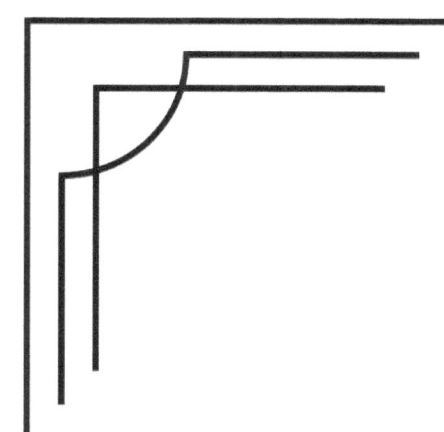

A change is long overdue

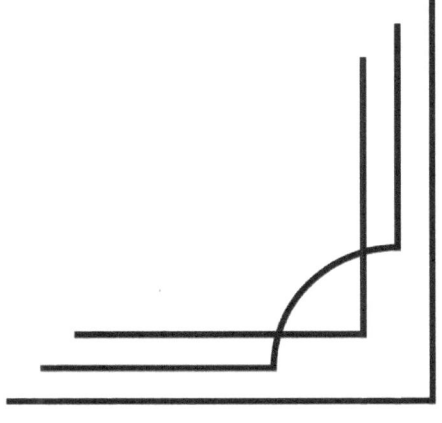

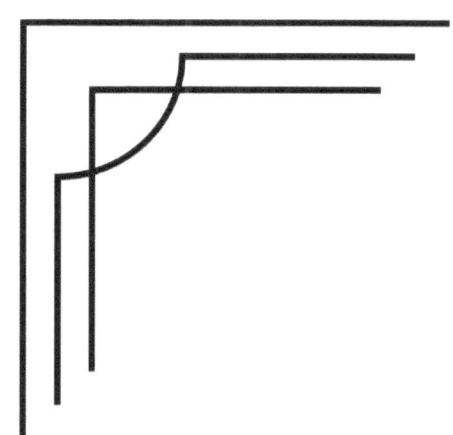

Don't waste your potential on this

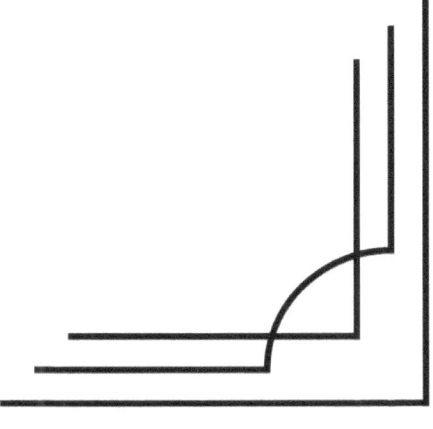

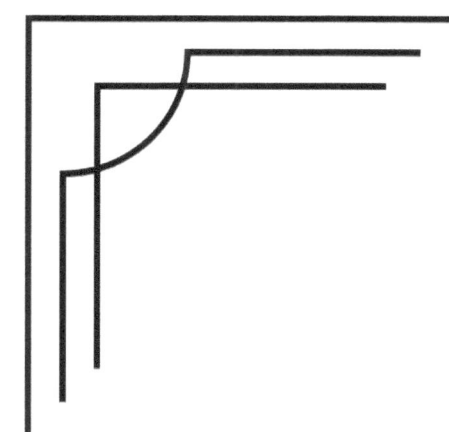

Watch and wait, it's almost time

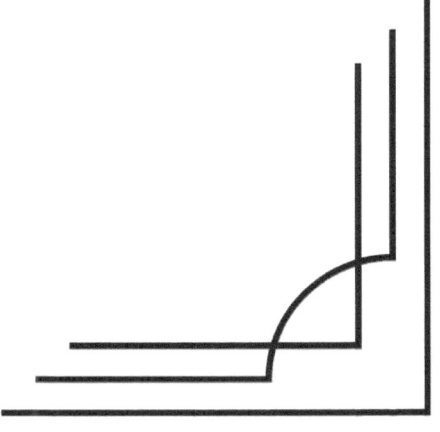

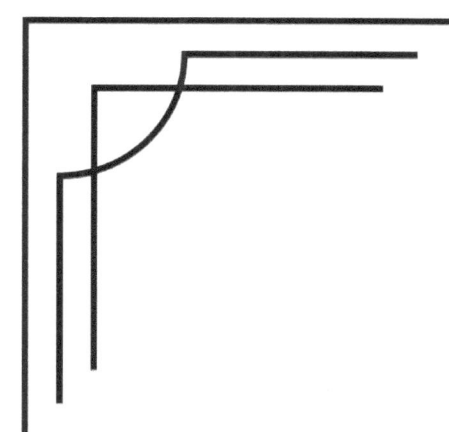

It's not time to deal with that right now

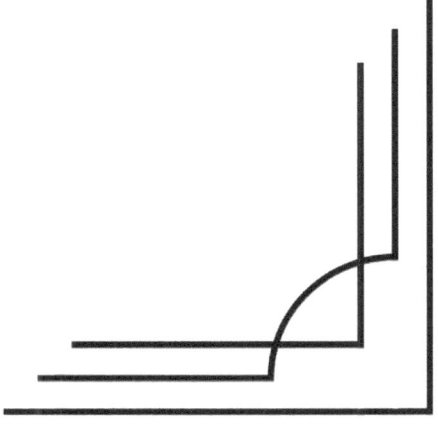

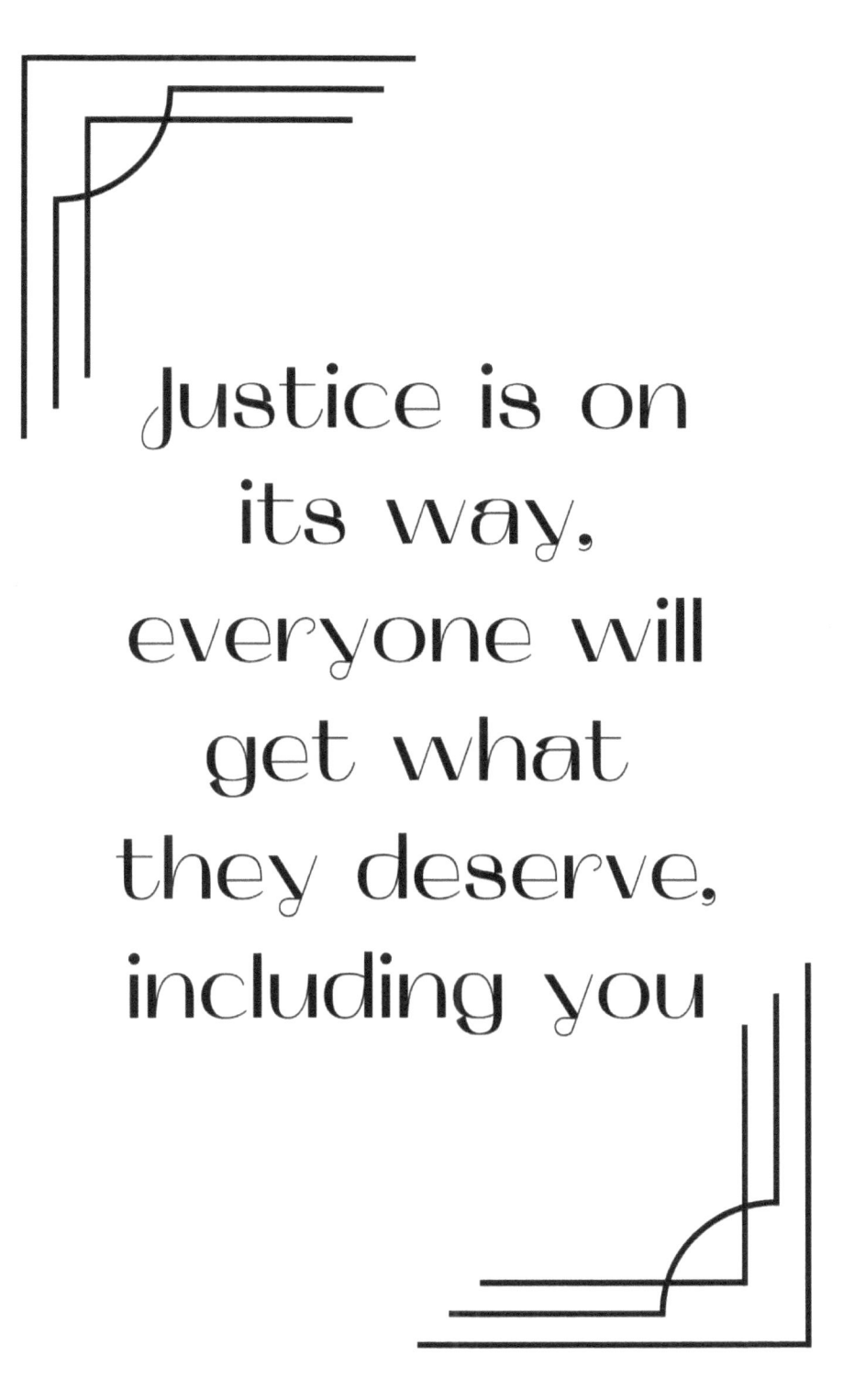
Justice is on its way, everyone will get what they deserve, including you

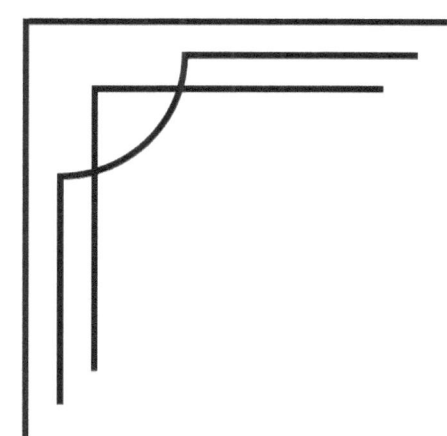

Acknowledge your role and act accordingly

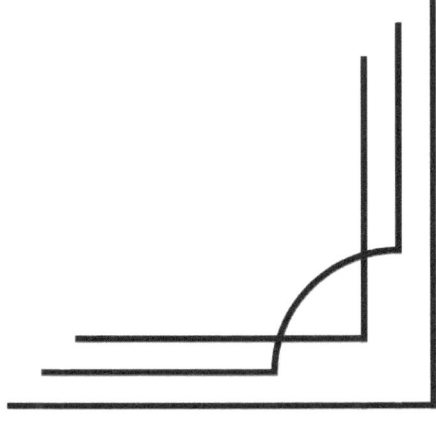

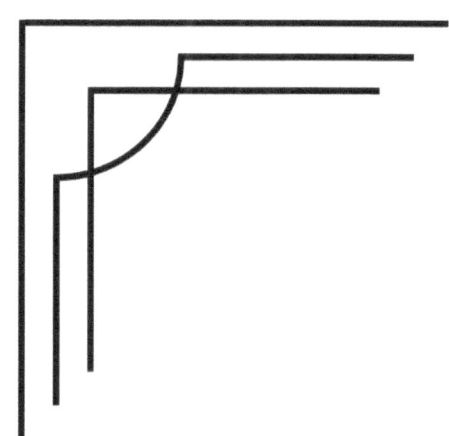

It's not for you

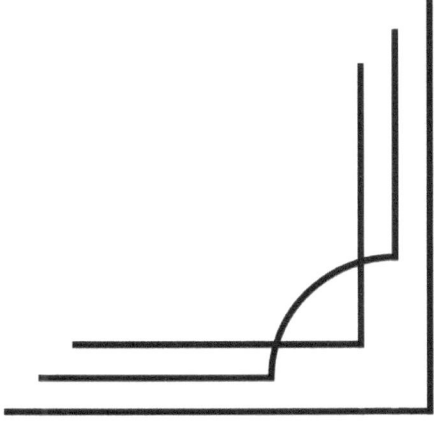

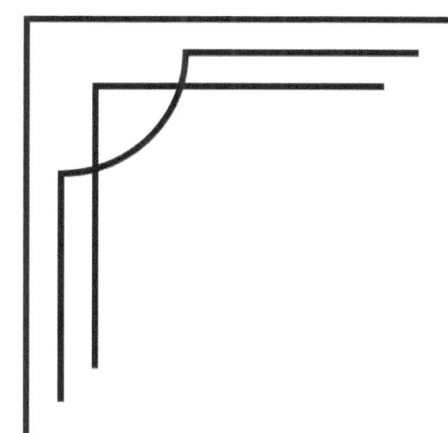

Ask again but on a deeper level

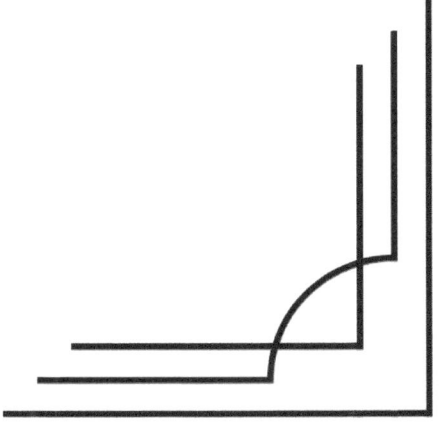

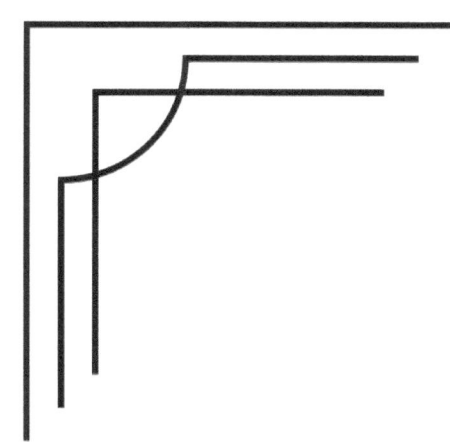

It's an easy yes

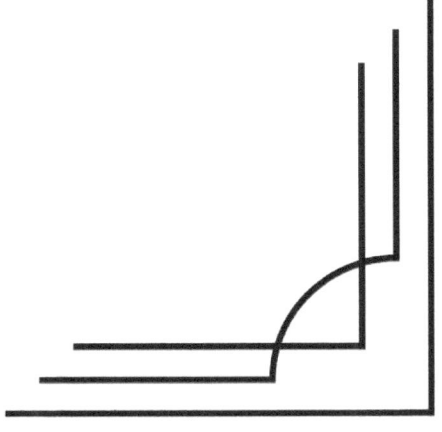

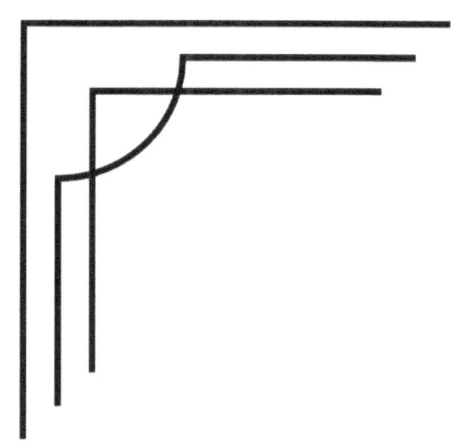

Take a chance on it

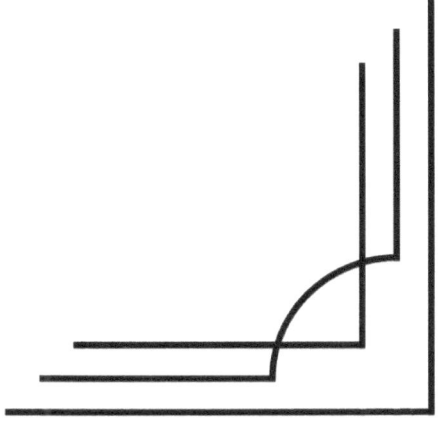

You can't keep doing the same thing and expecting a different outcome, even a slight change can have a massive impact

www.ingramcontent.com/pod-product-compliance
Lightning Source LLC
Chambersburg PA
CBHW030259100526
44590CB00012B/446